TJ CLEMONS

Pimp Game 203

Pimping Aint Easy

Pimp Game

203

Pimping

Ain't

Easy

TJ Clemons

itbftr@yahoo.com

Introduction

Once you make up your mind to jump into this game, then you have to

know everything that comes with it, because pimping ain't easy.

The whole world is basically against you, and you really have to make

sure that your girls are down for you from day one, because they can

either bring you up or tear you down depending on what moves that

they CHOOSE to make on your behalf.

They represent you daily. And people are going to try to change their

minds about you every day. They are going to try and TRICK them into

going against you and your philosophy constantly.

 It's a mind game that they are trying to play against you and your belief

system. They are going to attack the KING through his QUEENS.

It is a very common tactic that is initiated in this game.

And you have to prepare your women for your opponents because your

enemies are going to be cunning as the snake in the Garden of Eden,

because they are constantly hoping and praying for your downfall.

Think of it as a daily chess game. They are coming to conquer your

kingdom to overthrow the King. So, every move that your QUEENS are

making should be in protection of their KING and vice versa. And you

must be prepared for battle every day, because the snakes and the

fakes are always on their way to try and take something from you,

including your life, your liberty, and the pursuit of your happiness.

Pimping Ain't Easy

I wake up every day with that drive and that dream to get out there and

I keep my mind on my money and my money on mind, while I stay on

my hustle and grind daily. My name is Money Mike and I'm here to tell

you from my own personal life experiences that pimping isn't an easy

task at all and the name of the game is to play or get played on.

Before I started getting any real money I had to survive every day.

I grew up poor, just like everybody else around me in poverty.

I remember sleepless nights going to bed hungry and looking forward

to going to school just to get a free breakfast and lunch meal.

People don't really know my humble beginnings.

They think that I just woke up one day and decided to start pimping.

If you really haven't been through any of life's struggles then you

really don't know how to pimp and manipulate just about any situation

to your advantage using only your mind and your mouthpiece.

It's a skill that I developed simply out of the necessity to stay alive.

I caught a whole lot of bad breaks in my lifetime. And I had a lot of ups

and downs, as well as bumps and bruises growing up in a poverty

situation. I got started in this game at 15 years old because I always

liked to dress up and have nice clothing.

I had already had my own car by then. My mind was already made up

that I wanted to be a pimp when I got old enough. Those well dressed

men in my neighbor who had fine women working for them bringing

them money was my inspiration, because in my mind this was the true

definition of success.

That desire to be a pimp was already in me at a very young age.

All the young guys in my neighborhood looked up to the street hustlers,

drug dealers, and pimps. And one day I wanted the ones growing up

under me to look up to me, and want to be just like me when they grew

up and started to get out there and start hustling.

I noticed these guys out there having women turn tricks and come back

and bring them their hard earned money. And I decided that it was

going to one day become my profession one day.

I recognized that I had those same qualities. Something way deep down

inside of me just knew that I had the talents to become a successful

financial manager of beautiful and exotic women.

The difference between dope dealing and pimping is that dope pretty

much sells itself. When you're pimping you have to have knowledge of

the game and the ability to attract, inspire, and guide women

throughout the entire process which sounds very easy but there are

definitely going to be some complications along the way.

All women don't have that ability, mindset, and attitude to want to

follow after a wise man who can offer them all the answers that they

are looking for to allow them to bring them into a situation where

he is going to reward them for their complete loyalty and dedication

to her comforter, lover, and protector.

You have to be able to enhance, persuade, and nurture the situation

that she pretty much already wants to be involved with.

It's a complicated and delicate balance. Women are very emotional

and they have to feel comfortable with everything that's going on with

in your relationship. But once she puts all of her trust, belief, and

respect into and you, and she knows that you're as down for her as she

is down for you, then the process and relationship will get better and

better the longer that all of those conditions continue to exist.

It took me a few years to really understand my position.

 I was initially looking from the outside into the game.

And when I finally got into it, I and got exposed to everything that

comes with it, then I knew this life was for me.

My attitude became pimp or die. I started believing in the pimp god.

I never really had a father growing up but the street hustlers became

my father figures. My father never came to support me in anything

that I was doing including me playing football or basketball.

I didn't really have a relationship with him until I was already in the

pimping game.

Apparently, he started hearing my name in the streets, and he

eventually came to me and let me know that he was proud of my

accomplishments, and for me being known as a respected pimp.

And I guess that inspired him to want to build a relationship with me.

My mother detested my chosen profession.

She was 100 percent against it.

She wanted me to finish school and go on to get a 9 to 5 square job.

I wanted to live my life for the game because I felt like the pimp god

was continuously blessing me to become better and better at pimping.

I thought people who went to work in the square world were mentally

deficient and something was really wrong with them for allowing

themselves to becomes slaves to the system of hard labor.

I already felt like I had a proper education with my GED that I got while

I was in the prison system. I had already had a felony so, getting a

regular job wasn't even an option because I couldn't get anything other

than a minimum wage position because of my record.

I had already figured out that I could earn better money in the streets.

So, this was the direction that I was headed in regardless of what she

wanted me to do. This was my destiny since childhood.

Nothing or nobody was going to stop me from pimping.

I had already been around pimps growing up. And I would see them

with their jewelry and fancy clothes. This was my realistic view of

my version of the American Dream.

I had already picked up some game from them and I was hungry for

more information and the street education to become just like them.

I was exposed to it at a young age, and I was already addicted to the

concept of having beautiful women around me giving me all of their

hard earned money from working on the streets.

I would go to a seasoned pimp and act like I knew what I was doing,

because I knew they would correct me when I was wrong, and educate

me on how to make my situation with women better.

I would pitch them my ideas on how I would manage my prostitutes,

and they would slowly but surely lace me with their street knowledge.

I would say stuff that I knew was wrong and completely out of pocket.

I started learning all about "the ism" which is pimp game wisdom.

I called it "shoplifting" which is basically stealing game from them.

The most women that I ever had at one in my stable was eight,

which can be a handful for even top notch players.

But I taught them all to get along like a family.

Over a period of time I figured out that one bad apple could spoil the

whole bunch. It only takes one female who has animosity and jealousy

towards another female to fuck up the whole situation.

And if I would see this going on I would pull her to the side and let her

know that her behavior wasn't going to benefit her or me.

I had to do this from time to time. And I had to let them know that

whatever the problem was that we are going to nip this shit in the bud

and fix it right away, because I just can't have reckless bitches fucking

up my organization or my mother fucking money.

Some people think that the game has totally changed over the years,

but I totally disagree. The game never changes only the players have.

There are some new guys with very different mentalities.

A lot of them are gang bangers. They are violating the game by getting

their women strung out on drugs and forcing them to do their thing

using violence and intimidation tactics.

This is not real pimping in my opinion because the same way that you

got your girl to choose you and agree to your terms and conditions,

then you have to keep that same energy with them.

You can't just switch up and expect her to respect your pimping.

It's just not going to work for your relationship with her in the long run,

because the next mother fucker is going to pull her from right up under

you because he is going to play on your mistakes and show her a better

option if she decides to change her mind about you very easily.

And before you know it baby girl is gone with the mother fucking wind.

I never try to get them with sex because the next mother fucker might

be packing a foot long sausage and break her back out.

Pimping is a mind game, because women can have sex with different

men all day and night long and keep bringing you money.

Making her climax physically isn't really that impressive because if you

get her mentally stimulated then everything else will fall in line

naturally and keep her around and wanting to be in your presence.

I remember being a rookie with one girl. She had injured her leg and

was on crutches, but she still wanted to go to work on the track.

She was putting in so much work that I was able to buy myself a

clean triple white Cadillac. After about 30 days her leg healed up,

and she was able to pull 7 more girls for me, while she was still on

 crutches limping around on the stroll.

She gave me the desire and motivation to do better because in my

mind having one girl was real close to having none, because anything

could happen with her at a moment's notice and I'm right back to

square one trying to figure out how to get another one.

The more the merrier if you ask me.

I didn't believe in putting my hands on my girls. It didn't really make

any sense to me because now she can't get out there or do her thing.

And now she is scared of you and looking to get away from you the

very first chance that she gets.

You can't send her to work like that and you're basically damaging

your own product and reducing the amount of money that she is

worth to a potential trick who might try to save her from you.

You have to have her there for you mentally, because the average

woman can handle pain. You can beat a woman black and blue

and it still doesn't guarantee that she is going to act the way that you

want her to act in any given situation.

They can stand outside in below zero weather without clothes on

with flip flops on and still go out there and make your money.

So, beating up on them really isn't going to accomplish anything.

You have to have some kind of control over their mind.

I threaten to fire one girl because she wasn't handling business

correctly. She wasn't producing or really making me any money.

I basically told her that she had to go so; I gathered all of her clothes

together and put them in my car and started driving towards the

greyhound bus station. I didn't really want to let her go but I had to

make her think that I was really fed up with her bullshit.

I told her to think about where she wanted to go because I was done

playing games with her.

You should have seen the confused look on her face.

It was fucking priceless. That bitch didn't really have anywhere to go.

And she really didn't have any other options at the time.

On the way to the Greyhound Bus Station she broke down and started

crying and she told me that she would get her shit together and that

I wouldn't have any more problems out of her.

And from then on there she made her mind up to go out there and put

her ass to the grind and she started getting money like a mother fucker.

The game will never change, only the players in it.

You have to get chosen with money. You can't do it for a promise.

I will respect the game though. If she chooses me and she is out on

bail, then I will give her pimp the bail money that he put up to get

her out. That is strictly out of respect for the game.

These new dudes aren't going to extend that kind of courtesy to you.

They will just snatch her up and keep it moving.

I look for intelligent females. I don't let my girls drink or get high.

Not while they are working anyways, because any kind of chemicals

dulls your thinking and you need to be mentally aware of everything

that is going on around you.

This is a very risky business and these females put their life in danger

every single moment that they are selling their bodies for you.

They are already targets for violence and abuse.

Some of these men try to kidnap and murder prostitutes.

They are already facing so many negative consequences just putting

themselves in dangerous situations with strangers.

They have to always be mentally alert and aware of everything.

But once you get off of your working responsibilities, then I don't

mind them having a drink or smoking a little weed to relax and unwind.

You don't want a girl who you have feelings for. You want her to be

always chasing after you and trying to keep you happy.

She can really have evil intentions for you if she feels like she can play

on your emotions or play any games with you at all.

Don't be falling in love with these bitches because

they are going to end up violating the game, bringing you bullshit and

nonsense all the time, and turning your other women against you

because you don't want her to leave you.

If you mess around with that type of foolishness, then you're going to

let a messy bitch fuck up everything that you have going for you.

When you have other girls that are really 100 percent down for you

looking at you like you have lost your mother fucking mind.

And eventually they are going to start looking down at you and your

pimping, and they are going to jump ship and look for another mother

fucker with a better plan than you're working with.

You can't have these bitches out here doubting you and looking at you

a certain type of way, because these type of females get easily

confused. So, don't even give them a reason not to believe in you or

your pimping because that right there is going to lead directly to your

downfall in this illustrious game.

Don't let these bitches get the idea in their head that they can violate

your rules and regulations because the next bitch around you is going

to follow suit and you're going to have a lot of chaos around you.

You can't be falling in love with these prostitutes and having them think

that they have the upper hand on you because they can and will play

with your emotions if you give then the opportunity to do so.

This game isn't about your feelings at all. You have to be cold as ice.

Women respect a man who stands up to his convictions.

They won't want to be around you if you fold easy.

You have to have your poker face on at all times, and let them know

that you're not a game to be played with. But, at the same time you

also have to know how to praise them when they are following your

instructions correctly. It's a very delicate balance when you're dealing

with the female species but once you have their respect and

admiration, then they will work their asses of for you.

It's a learning process, but you will pick up bits and pieces along the

way as you spend more and more quality time with your women.

I want my women to like me and not want to be with anybody else

except me. I don't like to count the women around me because what

I'm more interested in is counting the money that they bring me.

I want to be able to measure money one day instead of count it.

I want have so much of it that I have to put it on a scale and weight

it to be able to figure out how much of it that I have.

The game is changing in some ways now. These new pimps are out

here trying to sell dope as a side hustle. They get mad when I call them

out on it because they are not really pimps.

They are dope dealers who are trying to hustle their women in case

they come up short and have to re-up on their drug supply.

It doesn't take a rocket scientist to sell dope. It moves hand to hand.

And it pretty much sells itself, especially if the quality is good.

But everybody can't be a pimp and be good at it because of all the

difficulty involved. Pimps will never be accepted by society.

They look down at men like me and try their best to crucify us.

Other pimps don't like you either because they see you as a threat to

them and their stable of women. And their women look at you like

competition to their men. This game is a rat race like a mother fucker.

When I interview a lady that wants to be down with me, I have to know

absolutely everything about her. I want to know if she ever snitched on

a mother fucker and got them locked up before.

I need to know if she gets caught up in the legal system if she is going

to go against me and make a statement against me.

I want to know if she is more loyal to me than she is loyal to herself.

I need to know if she has any connection to law enforcement.

I need to know if she is on any kind of psychological medication.

I want to know if she is pregnant or if she already has any children.

I need to know everything I can about her before I send her out

there on the stroll to represent me and all of my interests.

You just can't accept any and every female. They have to meet certain

criteria and qualifications, because all money isn't good money.

Any one of these females can put you in a situation to either

lose your life or spend the rest of it locked up and away in a cold dark

place away from everybody else in society.

When I first started there weren't even any pagers around.

You had to be a doctor or a lawyer to have a pager.

My girls used to call me from pay phones to pick them up.

We thought we had it going on when we finally ungraded to pagers.

Now they have to computers, the internet, and cellphones.

These mother fuckers have it easy as fuck today.

We used to have to ride up and down the track to find our bitches.

And hopefully she was still around sometimes because they jump in

and out of cars all mother fucking day and night long.

We had to ride around and check on them. Now all you have to do is

send her out a text message and know exactly what is going on with her

when she gets a chance to hit you back.

And these mother fuckers don't even trust their women because they

have to run up on them as soon as they jump out of the car with a

trick to get their money. We never had to do that back in the day.

I collected my money at the end of the night.

I don't want to get caught up hanging around the track and having my

girls keep handing me money. That constant hand to hand money

exchange can easily get you caught up with a very serious case.

Somebody might be out there building a case on you and they will

easily have that information on you if you're constantly around her.

You're just building up more and more evidence against yourself.

You can't be out there in public or on the track communicating with

your women on a consistent basis.

I had to move around a lot because these tracks are very small and

attract haters very easily. Even though you grew up with these guys

and you know them from the streets, you can't trust them or give them

any opportunity to try and knock you off your hustle and grind.

You always have to remember that this is a mother fucking rat race.

And all of these other rats are competing for the same cheese you are.

I'm not hating on the new guys, I just have more in common with the

old school hustlers who came from where I came from and they know

the struggle from a very different perspective.

We basically paved the way for this new generation of hustlers.

Some of them give us our proper respect, while others choose not to.

When we come around some of them back up and recognize game.

Some of them are absorbing, sucking up, and stealing game from us.

Like I said before, the game is still the same only the players change.

Pimping is like a cult or a secret society.

It's lonely at the top. It's a very lonely game because society won't

accept us for being something different and special.

They see us dressed up making a living like we choose to do.

I have nice cars and beautiful women making large amounts of money.

They never see me doing anything and they keep trying to figure me

out because I'm doing pretty well for myself.

I live a very different lifestyle. Most of my neighbors are out working

all day and my cars are parked in the driveway. Then when they get

home from work, I'm getting ready to head out to work all night.

Some of them actually started leaving notes on my car requesting

cocaine and different kinds of drugs because they thought I was a

dope dealer with a good connection.

It actually started getting annoying to me because I was trying my

very best to keep a low profile.

I got so frustrated that I called the police and asked them what to do.

And they told me next time I got one of these notes to bring it in to

the local police department. So afterwards I got one of these notes and

I drove to the police department which was only a few blocks away.

I gave it to the officer at the desk and he looked at it.

Then he asked me how I got there. I told him that I drove down there.

He then informed me that I was under arrest for driving while under

suspension because my license wasn't completely legit or valid.

The whole time the cops knew what was going on because they

basically were the ones who were leaving the notes on my cars.

They was trying to find out what kind of street hustle that I had going

on because I was living in a nice neighborhood with nice cars and

they couldn't verify my source of income.

I check out females and look for the qualities that I can work with.

A lot of people think that we are forcing women to sell their bodies

against their will, but it really doesn't work like that in most cases.

If I have to put my hands on my girls then I don't need them.

They are naturally curious when they see a well-dressed man.

I can tell by the way they look at me in my luxury vehicles that they

are interested in starting a conversation with me to see exactly

what I have going on and what I can do for them to be down with me.

It's a very natural attraction that needs to be satisfied within them.

And then I pretty much check them and see if I can work with them.

I usually go with my natural feelings about them before I interview

them for a position with me.

I talked to them and get to know everything about them as I can.

If they start talking crazy or reckless, then I move on along.

Pimping is one of the hardest cases to prove but if you give a woman

a reason to turn against you then she is going to go out of her way to

use all kinds of ammunition against you. Then it's all bad for you.

She is going to have something to work with. And you're going to

get jammed up in those set of circumstances.

Never beat up your woman and send them out to work for you.

They are going to hold it against you. And women are already

emotional creatures. And she is going to start plotting against you.

Sometimes you have to check them before you send them out.

But if she can't tell you exactly what she did wrong in the situation

before she leaves your presence then you're going to have problems

with her without a mother fucking doubt in my mind.

So, what I do now after I check one of my females I interview them.

If she lets me know what she did wrong, and why I had to talk to her

about my rules and regulations, and why she was wrong in the

situation, and she can explain it to me clearly then I'll send her back

out there to work. I need to know that she is down with my program

and wants to freely move forward with my organization.

I can't with a clear conscience send my women out there with any

kind of attitude or having any kind of problems with me.

That can lead to a minor misunderstanding between me and her

causing me to get locked up. Because in the wrong mental state of

mind, she can and will say something wrong that can get me locked

up for a very long time. I have enough experience to know to get

things right with our relationship and keep it that way.

She can get locked up and those funky mother fucking vice detectives

can sense or "detect" that we have something negative going on

between me and one of my ladies.

And try to use that information to fuck with her mentally. And in a

moment of weakness, she can easily say or do something stupid that

can fuck up my situation. My girls already know that I'm 100 percent

down and I'm coming with their bail money if they get caught up in

some legal bullshit. I'm not going to leave them hanging.

It's my responsibility as their man to be there for them and take care

of anything that comes up in the process of getting our money.

I already gave them my word as a man. And I always come through.

If they are handling my business then, I' m damn sure handling theirs.

These married men are out here shopping for my girls every day.

And I manage their activity. I teach them how to hold conversations

 with these guys on any level that they are going to be approached.

I'm a coochie coach. There is a demand for them that has been

around since the beginning of time.

These married men aren't getting what they want at home from their

wives and girlfriends. And I'm here to provide them with the type of

fantasies that they are looking for with my women.

They get to do it stress free with no worries or nagging from a woman.

They have so many bills and responsibilities that they can't even get an

erection without having an argument at home.

My women are going to love on him and make him happy for a small

fee, and he is going to keep coming back for that erotic experience.

She is going to help him release all that pressure and be able to deal

with all the bullshit that life has to offer him every day.

He is going to get his sexual fix and ride off into the sunset with a smile

on his face and a glide in his stride. And they are going to give me

the reward of their hard labor after he goes in his pockets.

They need me to be there and manage their money for them.

They don't have the motivation or the mindset to manage money.

And that's where I come in to take care of them.

I remember rolling up on a couple of my ladies after they had messed

up all of their money instead of checking in with me.

They should have both had at least a thousand dollars for me because

in my mind they belong to me until I get a phone call or something

and find out something different or they chose another pimp.

And when I rolled up to check them, they only had about $100 between

the both of them. Without a man to properly manage them, they would

have been satisfied with that amount of money.

But with a man like me inspiring and motivating them and showing

them a better way, then they can do a lot better with me than without

me giving them that push in the right direction.

I try to make my women look better than any other girls on the track.

I dress them up to attract attention and money from their tricks.

It also attracts other females to me because they want to look good

while they are outside in the public eye. Success breeds success.

Square mother fuckers don't understand anything about this lifestyle.

They don't comprehend how I can have sex and make love to my

women any way that I can imagine and still be able to send them out

to sell their bodies to other men for money.

And these tricks get mad because the only way that they can get my

women to get freaky with them is that they have to pay for the

satisfaction of experiencing those same pleasures.

That is exactly why square men can't stand a pimp mother fucker.

I used to feel the same way about them, because they can't accept

me in their society yet, they want the pleasure of playing with my

beautiful women when I allow them to do so.

It's pretty much a mutual thing. But I do enjoy spending their money.

It's all about jealousy and envy. Even other pimps are guilty of it.

Jealousy to me is a sickness and disease. I want everybody around

me to be successful, the tricks, the squares, and the pimps.

Success is what motivates me not failure. I want the finest things.

The only thing that I have a problem with is these part-time pimps

who are trying to sell dope and pussy at the same time.

If you want to sell dope then sell dope.

I'm not hating on them at all. Do what you do. It's just sad to me

because any and everybody can't be a pimp.

I have never been in love before. But I really care for my women.

I would have died for them in certain situations.

I don't know if you call it love or not but if one of my girls are on the

track and a mother fucker tries to violate them or put them in any hurt,

harm, or danger then I can't just sit there and just let that happen.

I'm going to do my best to get that mother fucker off of her.

I don't know if this mother fucker is packing a knife or a gun but

I have to do my best to protect her. That's why she is paying me.

 I can't let her get killed on my watch. I put my life on the line

the exact same way that they are putting their life on the line for me.

I am a man first, even before I am a pimp.

I don't demand respect. I command respect.

I'm going to respect you the same way that I want you to respect me.

If you're not giving it to me then, I will demand it by any means

necessary for me to get it from you.

I'm either going to knock you down or you're going to knock me down,

but either way, you're going to respect me at the end of the day.

When it came to my girls, any and everybody couldn't be around me.

I'm not going to have you around me just because you have a mouth

and pussy and know how to use them to get money.

I want their tricks to get an intelligent conversation that he can't even

have at home with his wife. That's the purpose of a prostitute.

He is supposed to get everything that he isn't getting from his wife.

It's real simple. Give that mother fucker what he is paying for.

I'm going to let my bottom bitch Goldie take over from here.

She is going to give you the ins and outs of the game from a female

perspective and point of view. I taught her well.

And she is going to finish off the rest of the way.

She has quite a story to tell so sit back and enjoy every moment.

Goldie

I met Money Mike and he brought me a very long way in this game.

I had two brothers that were pimps so I was exposed to the game early.

I learned very fast not to let a boy kiss you or have any kind of sex.

And sooner or later they were going to go in their pockets to try their

best to impress a young lady. And if I did decide to give them some

play, then they would be too embarrassed to tell anybody that they had

to pay to get some pussy from me.

That's sounds crazy but I was absorbing all different kinds and different

levels of the pimping game from my own perspective as a female.

I heard my big brothers telling their little whores certain things.

And I'm just sitting back watching it all go down every single day.

The game is in me and not just on me.

I was in the 7th grade the first time I gave a boy a kiss for $50 dollars.

I was 20 years old before I really started getting down on a sexual level.

I was little gold digger when I was a little girl. I always wanted money.

If you couldn't buy me anything, then I didn't even want to talk to you.

Money is a very important part of my life and getting to know me.

Socket to a bitch pockets, fuck falling in love and that other shit.

I'm married to the game and its purse first.

I was with Money Mike for years. He got me from this older guy.

I was young and very happy to get with Money Mike's pimping.

He was fun, exciting, interesting, and very well dressed all the time.

He already had money, cars, and a whole lot going on.

It wasn't like I was starting off with nothing. So, I was instantly down

with him and his program. I was excited by it, and I wanted to be a

part of his organization as one of his bitches.

I got a lot out of it and a lot of game along the way and intelligence.

I learned a lot. If it's not a blessing then it's a lesson.

He made me a better bitch and a better person. Some of these women

are out here fucking for free and all kinds of shit for their men.

I can go to sleep good knowing that I got paid for my pussy.

And I always use protection.

I had a few run in with the law but I also knew how to swindle my way

out of trouble. And when I couldn't, Money Mike never left me in jail.

He is coming to bail out all of his bitches without a fucking doubt.

I have a daughter who is grow now and she respects the game.

This wasn't the path that she chose to take though.

I always kept her in private schools and she had the best of everything.

Eventually she found out how I was making a living.

It became normal to her because she knew I was taking care of her.

I was always around players, pimps, and hustlers.

We lived in good neighborhoods and drove around in luxury cars.

She knew something was jumping off, but she also knew to stay in a

child's place at the same fucking time.

I'm retired now and I'm a Madame. It's not like I'm a pimp.

I just charge them service fees for accommodating them with clients.

I would never claim to be a pimp.

It's an addictive lifestyle though. The game keeps calling my name.

You have to know when to give it up though and move on.

I left out the game gracefully. I didn't want to be one of those females

that didn't save up money for a rainy day and have to keep going on

way past their prime. But at the same time I don't knock them for

still doing what I used to do. I can't judge them for grinding.

Because I ate and lived off of that prostitution money for years.

And it's good money if you manage it well.

I never did any drugs or got strung out on anything.

I drank liquor some times and smoked weed and kept it moving.

You always want more money though. There is never enough.

I'm retired, but if I happened to come up on a rich mother fucker,

I would gladly give him exactly what he is looking for.

I got that sunshine. I never had a problem satisfying a client.

And for the right amount of money I would make that mother

fucker's head spin around right now. And I bet he would want my

number to get some more of this sweet goodness that I have.

There is something about this lifestyle, with men willing to pay

you large sums of money to be with you that makes you feel

special in a different kind of way that I can't really explain.

It's a vanity thing. It makes you confident, not really conceited.

It feels good when you still got it. Young boys still try to get at me.

I'm a fox not a cougar though. They can get some wisdom from me.

I'll treat them more like a nephew than a lover.

I don't play those types of games with young men.

I'm way too sophisticated for that bullshit and drama.

You have to worry about getting robbed while you're working.

Some women lose their minds and their own selves in the process.

I only get depressed about poverty. I'm a very happy individual.

I just don't like being broke.

Prostitution has been going on since the beginning of time.

And it's never going to stop. Only the pimp god can take a prostitute

out of the game and move her in a different direction all together.

It's a doggy dog world. Eat or be eaten alive.

I don't have thin skin. A lot of women can't live this lifestyle.

A lot of men as well as women can't handle what comes with it.

There are a lot of extra ordinary people in this game.

I came up on $500 my first time turning a trick and I was hooked.

That's worth about $1500 dollars now.

I seriously thought that I had discovered something new and exciting.

I was in a stable with mostly white girls. I was the only black female.

I really benefited around being around snow bunnies though.

I found out a lot of valuable information and perspectives from them.

I remember getting so much money from this prostitution game.

I had tricks lined up waiting to get with me. They looked for me.

And they wanted me like they wanted the air that they breathed.

I was a happy hooker. I had fun with Money Mike.

And he made sure that all of his women were dressed up head to

mother fucking toe looking like fresh money that just got printed.

It really built up my character and enthusiasm for working.

Money Mike had us all in different motels.

He had a first, second, and third string of women based on how much

money that we brought in for him, but he made us all feel special.

All of them weren't good looking like me but they had talent.

I was a starter and I never warmed the bench.

I'm pretty but I'm also dangerous. I know how to throw hands.

I got really sick on the stroll one night. I was scared for my life.

I was pregnant at the time and had some severe pain.

I ended up having to have emergency surgery and they left surgical

sponges inside of me. I almost died from an internal infection.

That was the worst experience in my entire life.

I had one trick pull a gun on me and I snatched it out of his hands.

I pointed at him and I really thought about shooting him.

I had some other close calls and one really crazy experience.

This rookie cop tried to arrest me and he looked inside of my hotel

room and I saw his gun and badge in the front seat of his car.

I took them both and hid them inside of my fur coat sleeve.

He pulled his car over to look for them and he tried to block me

because you could only open the back doors from the outside and

I ended up pushing him out of the way and I ran off with them.

I kept his shit and jumped on the first greyhound bus out of town.

I think he got demoted or fired for that mishap.

I'm a happy hooker though. Money Mike had some good pimping.

And he was really good to all of his women.

We had nice cars and nice places to live.

Sometimes I regret not taking opportunities from movie producers.

I am a very attractive lady and I have a very witty personality.

I was offered so many different roles and television appearances.

I was too sprung on Money Mike's pimping and that was against

his rules and regulations.

I never fell for the bullshit from tricks who tried to save me.

They offered to help me with this and that. And they couldn't

understand that I had a pimp to pay and that was the only thing

on my mind back then.

I was in love with my pimp's dirty drawls.

He had a lot of women and he treated us all like queens.

And we all knew not to be jealous of each other.

I couldn't stand tricks, but I was nice to them just to get my money.

I was always happy when it was done and over with.

This lifestyle was my destiny. It was already written.

And I sprinkle these little young bitches with the game.

Nobody told me anything. I had to learn from the bottom up.

I tell them to stack their money up and have a plan to get out.

I tell them to stay away from drugs and to always use protection.

I have never been robbed but a few tricks tried me.

They never succeeded though.

No weapon formed against me has ever prospered.

Some mother fuckers tried to kidnap me but I made them crash.

I was kicking and screaming.

There weren't going to drive me to my death.

That was a scary experience but I walked away from it.

I lost a heel but they didn't get me or my money.

You can't be slipping like you have banana peels under your feet.

There are top notch women that can get it places that others can't.

They have females that are on the track that are comfortable with

that situation and they don't even want to elevate into something else.

Those women have a mentality that if it isn't broke then don't fix it.

And they know how to get good money on the stroll.

Every female is important because they play a role in the organization.

There are lessons and blessings going on every day in the game.

I'm very passionate about this game.

I wasn't looking for it but it found me. It was my destiny and fate.

I was just there at the right time and place for it to touch me.

A lot of square mother fuckers have their own perception of this

lifestyle but I look at is as the only way of life that I have ever known.

They think that every pimp is a man that looks down on women.

And that he is a piece of shit scum of the earth type of mother fucker.

And that they make us feel like less than we actually are.

It's a whole other world from my perspective because Money Mike

was there to build us up, not tear us down. I was very happy hooker.

There is way more to it than it is represented to be.

I wanted to be a prostitute. And that's the reality of it.

I used to see my brothers bitches and they were so fucking fly.

I wanted to just like them. I didn't want to be a punk ass bitch.

Pimps talk down to these types of women because they don't step

their game up and move accordingly like he gave her his game.

I wanted to be a top notch bitch in this game.

I wanted to shine and get praised by my pimp for living up to his

expectations and exceeding them every chance that I got to.

I wanted to be a product of his pimping.

I use to see and hear a lot of things growing up.

I remember my brothers blessing my mom with money regularly.

I looked up to them for handling their business like grown men.

And they gave me a lot of game along the way when I was coming up.

One of my older brothers died at a young age but he gave me so much

knowledge about life and everything that was going on in the world.

He told me how to handle myself as a young lady.

 I knew better than to go around giving my pussy up for free.

I knew I was more valuable and worth more than just money.

He taught me how to break men for money and he knew that they

wouldn't talk shit about me if they had to trick with me to get it.

And he told me that they would come back with more money if

they wanted to get with me because I was more than just a pretty

face. Now they started to find me irresistible.

My pussy became an investment opportunity in my mind.

I learned how to get the purse first.

Because once a man gets off then he isn't thinking about you.

I wanted that money and I definitely knew how to get it.

These young bitches are caught up in social media.

Most of them are pretending to be something that they are not.

It's like witchcraft to me.

Prostitution is part of god's plan.

You can find more loyalty in a whore house than you can in a church.

And we are choosing to do this by choice and not by force.

I'm going to keep it 100 and funky with you.

I have seen a pimp change a bitch's life for the better.

I'm talking about real pimps not the hoe hustlers.

Nobody around her life situation may not have anything going on and

all she really has to survive with is her mouth and pussy.

It's time for her to either hoe up or blow up.

And she feels like a celebrity when she comes back every three months

and blesses everybody around her because she was out there with her

pimp correctly handling her business.

A lot of females get into prostitution because they were either

molested or they started doing drugs and they had to support their

habit. That's not the case with me.

I saw the game from a different perspective all together and I wanted

to be a part of it with something way down deep inside of me.

I saw well-dressed men with nice cars and I wanted to get with them.

It looked very glamorous to me. I watched my brother give my mother

so much money and they really took care of us.

I had it real good. And I saw all of their beautiful hookers all dressed

and looking like movie stars. They didn't discriminate. They had all

kind of nationalities working for them. Every female had a position.

It was exciting for me and I wanted to get down when I grew up.

Some females just aren't built for this game.

They couldn't even get a trick to buy them a Happy Meal.

It's all about looking good and believing in yourself and your abilities.

Every prostitute is important and plays their role.

Eventually they learn the game and advance accordingly.

There is always room for elevation.

The top notch females work hard for their position with their pimp.

You can't just sit back and watch and not learn anything.

You have to step up on all ten toes and make something happen daily.

You have to be an example to the females that are underneath you.

I came into the game a top notch bitch.

I knew how to boost nice clothing, so I stayed fitted and looking good.

I looked like a movie star my first day on the stroll.

The other bitches thought that I was a cross country veteran.

I was a well-dressed good looking turnout.

I had a cigarette in my hand strutting like a mother fucking peacock.

I was 20 years old acting like a grown bitch.

I had been breaking mother fuckers for money so I had experience.

I knew black men wanted to just hit it and quit it.

And all the other men fantasized about being with a pretty black girl.

So, that is who I went with as tricks.

I knew how to look at the big picture. They used to take me shopping.

I used to model my outfits for them at the stores like a Barbie Doll.

I had them mother fuckers all the way in check.

I turned out with two snow bunnies that were top notch bitches.

I was asking for $100 when the other bitches were settling for $50.

That was big money back then. I was getting white girl money.

I looked like money so the tricks knew that they had to pay up.

They had to pay for the pleasure and the prize.

I needed money and my job just wasn't doing it.

So, I got with some girls that I knew were getting big money.

I knew what they were doing to get it and I got with them.

I only planned on doing it one weekend.

But one thing turned into another and I fell in love with the game.

I ended up meeting my first pimp who was a finesse type of pimp.

He was real cool and calm with me.

He treated me so good then he got sick and ending up passing away.

Then I got with Money Mike and it was a whole other ballgame.

I could take all the game that he could give me.

And I wanted more and more game every single day.

He put me to the test and I kept achieving more and more.

I put all my tools and jewels to work for him.

Sometimes he told me I wasn't working hard enough.

And I felt like he didn't understand all the work that I put in for him.

That motivated me to step my game up even more though.

This game has been around since the beginning of time.

And it will be around until the end of the world as we know it.

It is a secret society of its own making.

It has its own culture and language.

And it has its own rituals.

Real pimps are blessed into the game.

You have to have money to get with a pimp.

You have to pay a choosing fee set by him.

Some of these men just think that they are real pimps.

They don't even have the knowledge and understanding of the game.

But you can't stop somebody from thinking that they know about it.

And they are going to go out there and pretend that they know shit.

And these weak-minded females are going to think that they know it.

I know how to separate the real ones from the fake ones.

If you been around it like me, then it's a lot easier to recognize.

But everybody doesn't know what time it is.

But anybody can fall for the okie doke.

The best game at the end of the day is yourself.

Everybody is different and they bring something different to the game.

You can take a little piece of the game from multiple people.

And you can go out and use it to the best of your own knowledge.

I can never be another person. I can land in another person shoes

and at the end of the day I'm going to move different in my journey.

It may be the same situation but the outcome is going to be different.

I'm going to be treated different or do something totally opposite.

We are all different people for a reason.

I wasn't ever forced to do anything. It was my choice to do it.

I wanted to be in Money Mike's organization and I loved being there.

He was a fly mother fucker and I wanted to be down.

We had fun getting money together as a team.

And I enjoyed being a team player.

It's totally different now. These new people make their own rules.

A bitch gives her pussy up for free.

And a prostitute like me gives up mine for a fee.

Hookers go other there and get their mother fucking money.

Some of these mother fucking bitches give it up now for a blunt,

some Taco Bell, or a small amount of drugs to survive.

Why would you give up your pussy for free?

That just bothers me way down deep inside of me.

If my husband doesn't get me what I ask for then that mother fucker

isn't getting any of this good ass pussy or get his dick sucked.

That cock sucker better recognize this queen that he is rocking with.

If he handles his business then I'm jumping off the chandelier and doing

cartwheels and land on his dick if he does what he is supposed to do.

It costs to be the mother fucking boss because I know how to please my

man without a doubt. I got that shit together.

I love my man but he better have some money if he wants to fuck.

I'm a happy bitch. I take lemons and turn them into lemonade.

I'm not a bitter bitch at all.

It's only 24 hours in a day and I'm not going to use them for negativity.

Some things in life are only a stepping stone to something better or

what you decide to make of it.

You also have to know and understand your value and your worth.

I want to be the first prostitute to go to the moon.

And I believe in my heart and soul that I can do it.

Pimps come to the urban areas and give women opportunities.

The game is getting watered down by want to be pimps and whores.

These females are out here doing something strange for a very little

piece of change that is barely even worth it.

I was in control of my tricks. They did what I told them to do.

We always had that one little nasty bitch that would do just about

anything that a trick told them to do but I wasn't that bitch.

I never fell in love with a trick only with their money.

I had a few that cut me off and I didn't like that at all.

I got served a few times and when they told me this was the last time

that I was going to get any money from them for whatever reason.

It's different culture of pimping styles in different area codes.

But at the end of the day it's a profession and we want to make

a decent living like everybody else. And if you don't have the same

resources as they do, then you have to use what you do have to the

very best of your ability to make it happen for you and the people

that are around you every mother fucking day.

Some people will never have certain opportunities and that is exactly

why we do what we do. Pimps pimp. And whores whore.

This is what the fuck we do because of the choices that we had.

I was taught from a very you age to never look down on what

anybody does to survive in this world.

Some people look at it different because they don't want their

mothers, sisters, or female relatives caught up in the game.

They think a mother fucker is pimp smacking them and making

them go out and sell their bodies to random strangers.

I'm not going to say that it doesn't happen that way.

Females get kidnapped and sex trafficked every single day.

But what I am saying is that it didn't happen to me.

That's not my story or experience as a working girl.

Pimps are needed in our society. They serve a purpose.

You have to open yourself to other people's lives and experiences.

You might not agree or approve of what they are doing.

But you can respect them as individuals doing what they want to do.

You can't tell everyone what to do with themselves.

You can't tell them how to think or feel.

The very same way that you can't tell them how to make money

using their own natural talents and abilities.

It's all about perspective sometimes.

But you will never be able tell anybody how to live their lives or

narrate the way that they choose to navigate in society.

Even stories or movies based on true life events are changed to fit a

certain kind of storyline so that the audience roots for the hero or the

main character for a dramatic affect.

People now a days do just about anything for clout or fame.

The game is really messed up. We need to do something to make it

great again. Quit calling yourselves pimps if you aren't pimping.

Stop being an imposter.

If you're going to do something in this game at least be good at it.

The game isn't for everybody. And some people just don't measure

up to the expectations of a real fucking pimp.

I came from a certain circle that everyone doesn't agree with.

But I was loyal and stayed true to the game anyways.

No matter what anybody thinks or feels about it they are going to

have their own perspective of what they think that this game is all

about. They have never even seen it up close a day in their lives.

They have only seen a representation of it from society.

They have the whole concept mixed up because they have no idea

what is going on inside of this secret society.

They try to make us look messed up but they don't even understand it.

I wanted to get all that money and travel across country to get it.

I just had that mentality to go out there and get that paper.

I was ready to put on my heels and flex for that money.

It's just in me to make something happen.

I'll be a happy mother fucking hooker until the day that I die.

I never wanted to be a pimp.

I don't like pussy but I respect the pimping.

I have been a Madame. I ran my own escorting service.

I never treated my girls bad or disrespectful.

I used to break for my pimp and give him all of my money.

But I don't do that with my girls. I only charged them a percentage.

I turned them onto clients for $1000 and charged a $300 fee.

They keep their money and there problems to themselves.

And they keep it moving. Because when you take all of their money

then you have take on all of their responsibilities.

And I wasn't going to be responsible.

It's a whole vibe.

You look at a woman for her beauty and what she brings to the table.

You can't take care of a woman that you can't come to any kind of

mutual understanding. It's just not going to work out.

You have be in love with your pimp to want to pay him.

Average women don't pay men average men.

I had to upgrade everything about me to get with Money Mike.

He didn't want and average bitch. I had to step my game up.

I was in love with that mother fucker and I knew how to show my love.

And I chose to do everything within my power to be with him.

Our Partnership Together

Money Mike: I was on the track sharp as a tack when I met Goldie.

I saw her looking good and pulled up on her told her that she was fine

like mother fucking wine. I liked her style and I just had to have her.

I kept talking to her until she jumped in the car with me.

Goldie: And I have been with Money Mike since that first day.

We haven't been together in the game for many years.

We have a mutual respect and admiration for each other.

I'm always going to love him but back then I was in love with

Money Mike. And I was in love with the game and his game.

I was down with his pimping and we traveled across country together.

I had so much fun and enjoyed it, when there were rules to this game.

Money Mike: Goldie is a Gemini, so it's like dealing with two women.

She went to work for me and really handled her business for me.

Our one on one relationship had a lot of ups and downs though.

People talk about the good times but don't bring up the bad times.

Our situation just lasted a long time and we're still cool today.

We do our own separate things now, but we still talk to each other.

There is a romantic element to these types of relationships.

It's not all about business all the time.

Goldie: I was in love with Money Mike. It wasn't all about him breaking

on me and getting my money. He is very romantic but you have to give

him your money first. You don't get all that goodness from him when

you first meet me and have an interview with him. You have to give him

some money if you want to see that softer side of Money Mike.

Money Mike: We had our ups and downs in the game together.

But once I put my pimping down on Goldie, then it got corrected.

And we still have an understanding today. I did right by my girls.

But if she left me, then she had to take everything with her.

I'm not running a mother fucking Storage Company for bitches.

Goldie left me a few times, but she always found her way back.

 I gave all of her belongings away because I'm a pimp and not a

rest haven or a Storage Company. I gave her shit away and she had

to start all over. Times have changed a whole lot though.

The game is nothing like it used to be.

Goldie: There are pros and cons to it though.

These girls have all different kinds of ways to get their money.

I was a street stomper. It wasn't that easy for me back then.

Strippers don't even have to have sex to get their money.

If they know how to work the pole and shake their behinds then they

can pull in bands based on their natural talent and ability.

I'm proud of them and I still sprinkle them with more game.

But it's messed up on the other side because they are using the

word pimp so loosely, and they really aren't pimping.

Money Mike: They use it like they are putting on a new pair of jeans.

Pimp this. And pimp that. Pimps used to have respect and style.

They are really using that word out of context. These pimps are

disrespectful which means that they are disrespecting the game.

Pimps used to dress up like entertainers and the whole nine yards.

Now pimps look like anything. They dress like squares now.

Goldie: It's being used as a dirty word in society. We are people too.

We are really part of a secret society. Not all pimps are out there

getting girls high off of substances and putting hands on them.

There are CEO pimps. There are finesse pimps.

 And they have pimps that are of every different nationality.

I hooked up with Money Mike because he was the CEO of his

organization and he had a vision. He pimp smacked me a few times.

But Money Mike has calmed down and became a financial manager.

Money Mike: I used to be detrimental to a bitch. I used to get in their

asses and I didn't care where I was or what was going on at the time.

If you disrespected me and my pimping, then I would put my foot right

in a bitch's ass right then and there.

But that was way back before OJ Simpson fucked everything up for us.

But now today before I put my hands on a woman, I would tell her to

gone ahead and get the fuck on away from me. Don't waste my time

and I'm not going to waste yours.

Goldie: I can name on one hand how many times that you hit me.

Money Mike: I'm not just talking about you because I had so many.

Goldie just outlasted all of the other girls that I had with me.

I had to put my pimp hand down sometimes to let them other bitches

know that I wasn't playing with them.

But none of them ever tried to call the police on me for putting my

hands on them because they knew that they were wrong and were

out of pocket. But these new bitches have 911 on their phones on

speed dial and they will send a mother fucker to jail expeditiously.

If a pimp would have smacked Chris Rock on live national television,

then that mother fucker would have went to jail right then and there.

Goldie: I'm not a bitter bitch like that. I'm a happy hooker.

Money Mike: That's the type of females that you want around you.

Goldie: I got tired of getting pimped on and started my own escort

service. But that didn't make me hate the pimping game.

The first men that I ever looked up to were my two brothers.

And both of them were pimps. I love pimps and the game as well.

Money Mike changed my life. He showed me how to manage things.

He gave me a lot of intelligence and information on everything.

Money Mike: I have never wanted a robot or a silly ass bitch.

I can't stand a stupid ass female.

They have to know how to navigate their surroundings and know

how to handle any and every type of situation.

I had one bitch that got me $500 a day. Her nickname was 500.

I want my females to know how to think for themselves and want to

move up and elevate into something better in the game.

Goldie: When I had new girls around me I stepped my game up

even higher because I wanted to be an example of what they could be.

Money Mike: I had one female who use to work with Goldie.

She called me a few days ago. She wanted to send me some money for

my birthday.

I told her that I appreciated it and that was some of the money that she

was making up for all of the times that she came up short with me.

We was sitting there on the phone cracking up laughing about it.

I don't want any bitter bitches around me or any salty bitches.

They will try some bullshit with you. They will try to extort you

and threaten to put a case on you. And police officers love sending

pimps away, especially for long periods of time.

I have some old friends who want to sit around and talk about what

we had going on back then and what we used to do.

But what I really want to talk about is what's going on with them now.

The average pimp is going to have a 25 year run. But at the end of the

day you still want your respect for what you contributed to the game.

I don't feel like I'm better than any other guy that's are retired from

pimping because I'm still out here. I feel equal to them if anything.

My career just lasted longer because I stayed in the game.

Goldie: Money Mike will give you the straight up truth.

He won't lie to you or try to sugar coat it or water it down.

And he is a very handsome man. That's why I stayed with him.

He always took care of business. I just went out and got money.

He did everything for me and I didn't have any worries.

Money Mike: I learned how to do everything and handle my business

correctly from an old pimp partner. He put me all the way together.

I watched him as a youngster and learned a whole lot from him.

I'm the best student that he ever had. He always told me that he

could pimp circles around me. He told me that he had bitches way

back in the horse and carriage days before cars were even invented.

Goldie: You can teach these new youngsters some real pimping!

Money Mike: I have had a few of these young guys ask me if Goldie

was still in the game. I told them to call her up and ask for themselves.

I can't speak for her I'm not her pimp any more just her friend.

Only she can tell you what she will or won't do for herself.

I know if a female comes and brings me some money for my pimping

then I'm going to give it to her if she knows how to listen and follow

my lead. Otherwise she is on her own because I make champions.

So, if you have some big money out there to offer her, then ask her

yourself if she willing to accept if for her services.

Goldie: I don't care how old that I get. I'm never fucking for free.

Quote me on that. You better break bread if you want some head.

Show me the mother fucking money. And I'll give you some honey.

Money Mike: It's my birthday today and we are headed to the

Players Ball to celebrate my success. And everybody still thinks that

me and Goldie are still working together. It's been quite a few years.

She hasn't given me any money in about ten years. I love her though.

And we are still cool and we still have each other's back when it comes

down to it, and I appreciate everything that she has done for me.

Goldie: He has been there for me. He was right there when I need it,

especially when my older brother passed away.

Money Mike: If any female that I have ever had on my team over the

years ever needs anything they can reach out and call me and I'll still

take care of it for them. I can't take it with me when I'm gone.

I even try to share this game with the young guys coming up.

I want to give it to them correctly so that they move accordingly.

If they don't want to listen to me then that's on them as men to make

that decision for themselves. If you don't like the information that I'm

giving you then don't listen because I'm going to give you straight up

game right from the horse's mouth. I'm going to keep it 100 with you.

Goldie: You're fine like wine because you only get better with time.

Look at me. I don't have wrinkles and I still have these thick thighs.

I love to love. And I still love this game. I'm trying to leave bread crumbs

for these young girls to follow and not make the mistakes that I made.

I want them to get all of their money. If I had all these avenues to get

money like they have then I wouldn't ever get any sleep.

Money Mike: I'm going to tell you the key to the entire game right now.

Your health is your wealth. It's all about living good and taking good

care of yourself along the way.

They still have to get where we are right now still looking good as we

do and be able to talk about their own journey and success in this

game. And I'm living proof that this shit isn't easy. Pimping is hard.

Goldie: I'm here to tell you that when you get to new levels that you're

going to meet new devils. When mother fuckers see you doing good,

it pisses off their whole soul. Accept the love and ignore the hate.

Money Mike: I have enjoyed this lifestyle with my women, and I

wouldn't change it for anything in the world. I have already made all

of my dreams a reality. And I enjoy helping young guys achieve it.

Goldie: I got so much knowledge and education from Money Mike.

I thoroughly enjoyed soaking up all of his game over the years.

Money Mike: I appreciate everything that you have done for me.

We are going to be friends to the end that were brought together

by this here game. You got the job done for me and I will always

give you two thumbs up for being a real woman.

Goldie: Let's get this mother fucking money then.

We really need to make a movie about our life together in the game.

Money Mike: My life has been totally insane but I loved every minute.

I have a few things in the works. A few people are very interested in

telling my life story. I move better on action than I do with words.

I don't like to talk about nonsense. If it happens it happens.

And even if it doesn't happen then I'm satisfied with the people who

know and love me knowing how it put it down in the game.

My name will ring in the streets forever regardless.

Goldie: I have this big personality and I want to share my story and

my life with the world, and with all the women that have gone

through what I have gone through in this game. I want to be their voice.

Money Mike: A lot of females have love for you Goldie.

Goldie: And I love them right back. And I keep leaving bread crumbs

for them to be able to level up in this game and get their money.

I want to make a movie about my life so that they can be captivated

by all of my real life experiences, especially the ones I had in the game.

Money Mike: If I could turn back the hands of time I would do

everything that I did all over again. And I would definitely send Goldie

back out there and represent me in this game all over again.

She is my idea of the perfect woman in this game to be with and she

will forever be my queen sitting beside me in this game.